PILLS
POETRY&
PROSE:

LIFE WITH SCHIZOPHRENIA

Rebecca Chamaa

Dedication

This book is dedicated to the following people: Marni Freedman, Jill G. Hall, Tracy Jones, Steve Kowit, Victoria Melekian, Suzanne Ward, Andrew Whitver, Joel Whitver (Vissia), and Matthew Whitver.

And, to my husband, Jean-Claude Chamaa, who is the love of my life. There is so much I couldn't do without you. You are more than my soulmate you are the breath I take. I love you beyond all words.

Table of Contents

Letter to the Reader

Dear Reader,

My one hope is that these essays and poems dispel some of the myths surrounding severe mental illnesses, and give insight into some of the daily struggles and triumphs of a person living with the disease, schizophrenia.

The essays and poems in this book were written over the past two years. You will find the essay, *The Birth of June* and the essay, *Overcoming Obstacles,* contain some of the same details. *The Birth of June* was written when I was first considering going public with my illness. It has a more questioning, terrified, depressed tone to it. I felt frightened and a bit defeated at the time I was writing it. *Overcoming Obstacles* deals with the exact same information, but after a year of slowly telling people about my diagnosis, I felt much more confident, and triumphant. I hope you will experience my new hope and successes as you move through to the end of the book.

The story of me, as a writer, is a sad one, but one I feel the need to share. When I was in my twenties, I was publishing my poetry, running a regular poetry reading at a theater turned coffee shop, and publishing a journal called, *The Numbug Ate the Passionate Woman with too Many Feelings for Lunch.* All I wanted from life was to be a poet and I was putting every bit of energy I had into becoming one.

That magical time in my life was very short lived. After I had my first psychotic episode, and was originally diagnosed with bipolar disorder, a psychiatrist I was seeing put me on lithium, and antidepressants.

I went through many medication changes and several different diagnoses during this time. The medications I was taking killed the desire to create and the ability to create. I found it impossible to read or write. I didn't have the necessary focus or patience for it.

Currently, I am on an antipsychotic medication combined with something for my anxiety. Although I know I will never be the creative young poet of my twenties, I am challenging myself to write. What is easy for others is often a struggle for me. It is a struggle, but I believe it is worth it.

I was once a young woman with a dream. I will honor that woman, and strive to achieve a piece or part of what she was capable of. I will reach back in time and take her hand. Although I don't recognize her in me anymore, she is my guide and I trust her. I miss her too. She was fearless, and passionate, and trusted the world and everyone in it.

All my best to you,

Rebecca Chamaa

SECRETS

Coming Out in Darkness

Last night I courted the universe,
fell in love with the wind and the waves.
My long hair down
I ran loose in its arms.
What I cannot say while shadows
are cast by the sun,
the night embraces
my secret unfolds.
I have told.
I have told.
And the night is still night
and thinks no more or less
of me.

Freedom of Speech

I've been silent so long I imagine my voice box with cobwebs. I feel like if I tried to speak about anything personal a small puff of dust would come out of my mouth instead of words. Twenty years of secrecy. Twenty years of hiding. Twenty years of pretending to be something I'm not. I'm not sane. Well, I am at this moment, but there is an ebb and flow to sanity that works its way through my thoughts throughout the day. I am never sane for twenty-four straight hours. At least, I don't think so. I've never timed it, but from experience I can guess that is true.

Maybe you wonder how someone who struggles with psychotic thoughts can present themselves as normal on a daily basis – silence and secrecy. Those two things can be misinterpreted by most of the people almost all of the time. People assume silence means you are introverted. They assume silence means you are thoughtful. They assume silence means you don't have a lot to say. I have so much to say that words are flowing up from my stomach like bile. I can taste them, but the lack of practice makes them stick in my throat like peanut butter with too little oil – thick almost to the point of causing me to choke.

Silence and secrecy aren't twins but cousins. Because I am silent, it is easy to keep a secret, or secrets about myself, my life, my experience, my diagnosis. Being schizophrenic carries with it a stigma that I've never thought I could live with. I am constantly bombarded with people making fun of those who hear voices. There is nothing funny about hearing voices. Voices can be terrifying. Voices can tell you to do things you wouldn't normally do. Can anyone who is not mentally ill really imagine having their own mind turn against them? Can they imagine having their own mind at war with itself? Can they really imagine their own mind wanting them to die? Only hell itself could be that scary.

Besides silence and secrets there are scars. How many misunderstandings have there been between in-laws and friends because I couldn't think clearly? I can't tolerate ordinary conflicts between people. Of course, that combined with my illness makes for a messy situation like lifting the beaters out of the cake mix while the power is still on and having cake mix swirl, twirl and fly across the kitchen leaving specks of batter on cupboards, counters and as high as the ceiling.

Did I say that I am tired? Scared but tired. I want to live my life out in the open. I want to be free. The fear of the stigma has imprisoned me for twenty years. It is as if I have been living part of a life. A life crowded by fear, covered in shame, and twisted with silence, secrecy and scars. Words are my way out. I need to find the first sentence. I am dying to find the sound of my voice saying, "I am mentally ill." I am dying to express my experience. I am dying for acceptance as I truly am, and if there is not acceptance to be had, am I any worse off? Am I any less alone? Will they hate me, or will they silently slip away not knowing how to treat someone who cannot be relied upon to always think rationally? I must find the letters that make up the words that will be my key to freedom.

What would true freedom be like? Would I laugh more easily at myself and with others? Could I share my psychotic thoughts with a friend and could we giggle? Good God, is that even possible? It sounds like hoping to win the lottery or something equally unimaginable or impossible – one in thirteen million. Could I get any respect at all from any of my in-laws? Would they just use this to further distance me from the family? Would anyone be able to put aside their own issues and see me as a human being with a mountain in front of me that I get up every morning and try to climb? It doesn't matter. Freedom doesn't rely on the thoughts of others. Freedom is being released from the inside out, and history has shown there is always a high price to pay for freedom.

I'm willing to pay the price. I know that it will cost my silence, cost my secrecy, cost my scars. I may be replacing old scars with new wounds. I don't know. I will be opening myself up to that dreaded stigma. I will be opening myself up to ridicule, judgment and assumptions. But I will be able to wake up every morning and face the world as myself – no hiding, no cowering, and no cover up. I will be whole in my imperfection. I will be able to begin to live life to the fullest without the fear of being discovered. I will be empowered by my honesty and courage. I will start this life over again as an adult, only this time I will be free.

The Birth of June

I have kept my secret from most people for twenty-one years. I'm ready to let it out. I don't know what the repercussions will be. Will my friends still call and invite me to Sunday brunch? Will my in-laws start excluding me again after all the years it took to get included? Will my husband's coworkers feel sorry for him? Will people judge me? Will they talk behind my back? I don't know the answer to any of these questions. I can't see into the future and worse yet, I can't see into the hearts and minds of people. I have to ride this road without signs. I have no GPS. I will arrive at a destination, or many destinations, and it will be a surprise. Negative or positive? I can't be sure.

In 1992, I was getting a divorce from my college boyfriend. I was a social worker for the State of Washington in Child Protection Services. Getting a divorce was emotionally trying, but at least money wasn't an issue. I made good money and could afford my own bills. Besides, I was good with money. I have always been good with money.

By 1993, she showed up. Her name is June (my psychosis), because I believe that was the month of her birth. She is nothing like me. Of course, we share the same body, but that is where the similarity ends. She doesn't love who I love. She doesn't think about God the way I think about God. In fact, she has thought she was God, well, at least Jesus, Son of God. She trusts no one. She is frightened, restless, and her thoughts come at her like the speed of an automatic weapon – rapid fire. She is difficult because she is so scared, and that is the core of it. She is frightened; frightened of the voices, frightened of the shift in reality, frightened of everyone and everything. She is hell bent on destruction.

June took over my mind for the first time a month before my family was successful in getting me into the locked ward of the psychiatric unit at St. Joseph's in Tacoma, Washington. The first few days she couldn't be in the general population because she wouldn't follow the rules. She tore the sheets off of her bed because she thought she was being drugged through the cloth of the bed covers. It was her first appearance so she didn't know why or how or what had brought her into my body and she kept trying to convince everyone that someone was drugging her. The hospital tested for drugs. She was clean.

As I write this, I get uncomfortable. It isn't just that my nieces and nephews will never see me the same way again, or that people may feel awkward around me. It is the remembering. The actual experience of having June take over my mind is so intense. I can feel a tinge of the heightened anxiety. I can remember that smells were so overpowering and made her paranoid. I can remember that she was afraid of everything and everyone and didn't even trust my mother. I can remember that before she visited, I was a woman without a mental illness.

When I was released from the psych ward that first time, June was gone. I was assigned a psychiatrist and he diagnosed the visitation of June as bipolar disorder. I was prescribed lithium and antidepressants. I went through a couple of years of frequent medication changes, and I quit my job as a social worker. I went through many boyfriends and I was mostly depressed. I started catering with my brother and doing other odd jobs. I bought a house in Tacoma, and my family helped me to fix it up. Aunts, uncles, and cousins came over to paint. The goal was to get my grandparents, who were currently living in California, and no longer capable of living on their own, a safe place to live. My family created an upstairs apartment for me and the rest of the house for my grandparents. By that time, I was on a low dose of Stelazine and Klonopin. It seemed to be working. There was no sign of June.

But she wasn't gone or done with me yet. She was lurking just off the edge of my psyche waiting for a time to show up. And show up she did, one fall day before my grandparents moved in. She was doing an art project in the upstairs apartment. She was going through mementos of my past, a boyfriend's old jacket, letters, a string of red beads. She was hanging everything on a bookstand with candles on every level. She was listening to the song, "Nothing Compares to You" by Sinead O'Conner. She kept turning the music up louder and louder and playing the song over and over again. It was as if she was working herself into a manic frenzy. She lit the candles, danced, and watched them burn. The jacket and papers caught on fire. The fire was too big for her to put out. I broke her spell and called 911 while running out of the house. June was gone. The firemen arrived and put out the fire, the upstairs was completely damaged. No one was hurt.

In 1997, the stress of living with my grandparents, working full time and the fact that I had stopped taking my medications brought a visit from June that was unlike anything before it. She brought voices, lots of them, and they directed June to do things, and she was unable to resist. I didn't realize they were friends of June's, I thought they were the voices of God or angels. They told her to drive my car and drive it fast, and she did, all over Tacoma getting rid of things that had sentimental value to me. She took a thirty pound bronze statue that my girlfriend, Jennifer, had made and put it in a fountain in front of an office building. The voices told June to drive to Bremerton, the town where I lived with my ex-husband, and where I had run poetry readings in the local coffee shop and met the poet, Marvin Bell, and dreamed of one day becoming a poet. I dreamed big dreams in Bremerton, and the voices wanted June to take me to those places, those places of dreams and mock me and my failures.

On the way to Bremerton, she hit a traffic jam and turned my car onto the shoulder of the road and hit the gas. She went soaring by the long lines of traffic unaware and unable to see what might be causing the traffic in the first place. She drove from Tacoma to Bremerton at speeds above the limit. Unfortunately, there were no policemen to pull her over and stop or slow her progress.

She drove to houses that I loved and had once dreamed that I might own; the cottage on the water that couldn't have been more than five hundred square feet that I called the, "Poet's House." She went to the old hospital where my office at CPS was when I worked there. The voices were taking her from one place to another through a town and down memories I didn't exactly want to relive. Then they, June's friends, told her to drive back to the Tacoma Narrows Bridge and jump off. She drove back toward Tacoma with the same high speed and recklessness that she had driven to Bremerton. She stopped my car in the middle of the bridge, climbed over the ledge and stood on a railing above the water below. She was holding on to a rail with her hands and balancing on the ledge with her feet. There was a voice that said, "Come on give me your hand." It wasn't one of June's friends it was a man, standing above her on the bridge. She lifted one of her hands to him and he pulled her back up to safety.

She drove my car back to my house. The voices told June to take all of my medication. She did. Then they told her to drive to Eastern Washington and jump off the cliffs into the Columbia River. June got back in my car and passed out somewhere on the side of the road between Tacoma and Seattle. Another stranger stopped his car, and stayed with her until an ambulance arrived. She was in and out of consciousness. I woke up several times with bright lights shining directly into my eyes and monitors affixed to my chest. People were talking to me but the fog was so thick I couldn't answer. In the morning, I woke up with a black substance all around my mouth (given to make me throw up) and June was gone. My parents came to get me and helped me get my car out of impound.

I am amazed when I think about this second episode of psychosis and realize that I am only alive today because of two strangers, two men whose names I will never know, who cared enough to save the life of a mentally ill woman. I wish I could find them. I wish I could thank them. I pray silently some times that their lives have turned out well and that they have received blessing beyond measure for stopping, for offering a hand, for dialing 911.

My family moved my grandparents into a nursing home because they realized the stress of working full time and taking care of them was too much for me. During this time June was mostly silent. I stayed on my medications and things seemed to go fairly well.

I am writing this at a safe distance, because it has been nearly seven years since June took complete control of my mind. I am married now and studying writing. Although June has been silent the majority of those years, I am reminded of her presence on a near daily basis. It is as if she lurks in the shadows of my life to remind me that insanity is not far for me. It is a dark and fearful world that June inhabits with her many friends. I am terrified of that world. I am terrified of June and her entourage. Keeping her silent is one of the reasons I don't skip a dose of medication or push myself too hard. Like I said though, June is with me. She is here when I am afraid to eat food that has been left out for fear that it is poisonous. She is with me when I don't trust people or feel safe with them. She is with me when my anxiety gets to a level that I have to be moving all the time and can't find a comfortable position or place no matter how hard I try. She is with me when I am walking in downtown San Diego and I hear and see people talking to people I can't see. They have their own visitors to battle. They are also hosts to the unwanted, and uninvited.

The next time June showed up I was living in Hollywood with my future husband. Every day, when he would go to work, I would rearrange the furniture. I made a bridge in the hallway out of stakes he had in the closet. I tossed coins all over the bridge like a wishing well that he would have to walk over when he entered the

9

apartment. I drew several drawings in colored pencil every day that Jean-Claude, my husband to be, thought to be brilliant. I cooked all kinds of breads, dips, and desserts and plated them like an artist. I made the living room the bedroom and the bedroom a studio. I made up dances and played the same music over and over again.

I had so much creative energy and it was coming out of me in every different direction. I also read the Bible. As with most times June appears, it is manageable at first, but then manageable turns to nightmare and things swing out of control with a ferocity that only locked wards and strong pills can contain. June became frantic with delusions and started walking. She became fearful of Jean-Claude. She walked one full day across Los Angeles in gang-torn areas. She stayed in a hotel. She went back to Hollywood the next day and found Jean-Claude and told him they must go to Seattle. He was terrified but agreed.

June and Jean-Claude drove straight from Hollywood to Seattle without stopping to sleep. They headed for a town in the Pacific Northwest called Ocean Shores, where my parents lived. My parents were not happy when we arrived in the middle of the night. My mother doesn't do well with June. She angers and frustrates her. We slept. June slowly subsided and I contacted my old psychiatrist and got a prescription for medication. As June slipped away at my parents' house, Jean-Claude drove back to Los Angeles because of work. We met up later in Oregon and he drove me back to Hollywood.

When I think of the terrifying times my husband has had to deal with June, a woman who is scary, who is unpredictable and who definitely doesn't love him, respect him, or care for him the way I do, I am amazed that he is still here with me. Thankfully, June hasn't been successful in destroying the best thing that ever happened to me, my marriage. She has tried though. Like I said before, she is hell-bent on destruction. The destruction of me and everything about me, around me, attached to me, that belongs to me, in essence she is trying to destroy all that defines me.

My husband and I moved to Burbank, a suburb of Los Angeles. We bought a condo, settled down, and I started seeing a psychiatrist regularly and taking my medication daily. I became very serious about my treatment at this time. June was silent for years. My husband and I built a life together. We both had jobs, and I completed a leadership training program. I was doing so well for five or six years that the psychiatrist decided that my psychosis had been brought on by trauma and that I wasn't really mentally ill. He took me off all medication. June was free.

The battle was to live through her escapades with as little damage as possible. She ended up controlling me for over six months. She nearly killed me again. I am now in treatment. I will never make peace with June. She is the face of my enemy, my own face. We battle each other in the invisible but powerful space inside my mind. On most days, I feel like I am winning. In any case, I have introduced her to you. She can no longer hide. She is no longer my secret. Maybe, that introduction will keep her from trying to overpower me and destroy my life. Maybe, an introduction was all she needed to release me.

Games I'm Good At - Strategy

I have mastered the art
Of keeping secrets
Most of my closest friends
And none of my husband's family
Know that I am mentally ill
My husband is a warrior
In the game
Keeping guard of all my symptoms
So they don't expose
My truth
We hide together
Holding hands
And whispering
Our bedroom
Is our sanctuary
Where we can talk
With total freedom
The rest of the world
We treat like a mine field
Waiting to explode

Coming Out in Light

She pulls the door shut behind her, the gust of wind lifting her hair. Kicking off her shoes, she moves swiftly through the house tugging at her pink Wyoming t-shirt, trying to get it off over her head. She unbuttons her skinny jeans after she tosses the t-shirt to the floor. Wriggling her legs and hips she shimmies out of the tight fitting cloth. Bra, panties, and socks create a colorful pile of blue, purple, and white. She turns on the shower and stands naked next to the curtain. She can smell her own sharp sweat. When the steam starts to come off the tile, she steps in. She takes the soap and sponge (scrubbing) her arms, her face, her stomach, her legs and down to her feet. Six months they have been dating. Tonight, she told him her secret (scrubbing), her diagnosis. (Scrubbing). Did he really ask if she was insane? (Scrubbing). He wanted to know if she would open fire in a movie theater or castrate him while he slept. Her arms and legs are red from the friction of the soap and sponge. *Voices? You hear voices?* He said. He didn't hesitate to say it was over. No kisses. No sympathy. No softness in his words. Her skin fiery red from scrubbing, she watches as the sudsy water spirals in the drain and is sucked down the pipes that she once believed led to the ocean.

CHILDHOOD

The Building Blocks of Silence

I could see my house from Grant Elementary School playground. That day there were no cars in the circular drive. I ran toward the slide that I slid down most days at recess. It was a tall slide, the tallest one I had ever seen. I grasped the metal railing with my gloveless hands. I was wearing green galoshes, my brother's hand-me-downs that kids made fun of, but that I loved because hand-me-downs made me feel like I had a piece of the person who owned them before.

I slipped slightly on the metal rung and my boots made a screechy sound. The rungs were wet from the morning rain. It was fall. I had on my orange coat, not down, we couldn't afford down, but an imitation. Still the coat was thick and well padded. As I climbed each step of the ladder, holding on tightly with my hands, it is possible that all I was thinking about was the placement of my feet as I moved slowly upward, but more likely I was thinking about something that happened in school, or that my parents would be home soon and the fighting might start, or my older brother might say something at dinner that made my dad mad and then the whole family would end up crying.

There might be violence. Violence was always lurking until it wasn't, until it was happening: loud, scary and carrying with it the possibility of people out of control. The wrong punch, the wrong twist, pushing on mom's windpipe too long, the leather belt swung too hard too many times on my brothers' bare skin. At the top of the slide, before I sat down, my foot slipped and I flipped over the railing.

I don't remember falling through the air. I only remember the loud thud as I lay on my back. My only thought was, "So this is what they mean by having the wind knocked out of you." I laid there until my breathing was normal. I didn't cry. I didn't run. I saw our family car turn into the driveway. I didn't tell them I fell-off the top of the slide. I learned early there was no comfort at home, and keeping secrets is the glue that holds kids like me together.

Rebecca Chamaa

The Ties to Siblings

It makes me feel warm knowing you
Remember dinners at grandma's and grandpa's house on Sunday
When grandpa would perform magic tricks
Pulling quarters out of our ears
And we laughed long after we knew that the quarter was tucked
In his hand
And churning ice cream
And polishing rocks
You also remember mom and dad as young adults
Because even though they were grown-ups and seemed old to us
They were barely in their thirties
And you remember me
Before schizophrenia became the enemy
So you are one of the few people who can discern
What is truly me
And what is a symptom of my illness
You don't look at me with those confused or startled eyes
When I say something that comes from a distorted thought
We can laugh about the tragedy of how an illness can sweep over a
mind
And try to kill the host just like a parasite
And the laughter can turn to tears in the best way
Because there is a kind of knowing
that gets more depth and flavor over time

When Dinner Bleeds

My dad wanted us to be tough.
For discipline he used a thick leather belt
and lots of Goddamns.
He wanted us kids to know how life worked
at least the way he saw it
all greasy, hostile and with women
who were mostly nothing but tits and ass.
He took my brother, Andrew, and me
out behind the house near the field
with one of our chickens.
We were eating peanut butter and grape jelly
sandwiches.
He made us watch while he grabbed that chicken
by the neck and started to whip it around
like preparing his arm for a baseball game.
He put the head and neck of that big white bird
on an old wooden stump, picked up an axe
and with one quick swing severed the head.
Then he let go.
The body of that chicken ran around in front of us
like a top spinning and spurting blood
for what seemed like forever.
My brother and I never ate chicken again
and our peanut butter and jelly sandwiches
were half eaten and left behind in the dirt.

Friend

We played on the monkey bars as children
Laughing
Hanging by our knees
We passed notes in the hallway in middle school
In high school we went to parties
With alcohol and boys
In our twenties we got married
And divorced
In our thirties we found new loves
New lives
In our forties we are like good books
With dog-eared pages marking our best passages

Runaway Years

I was neither ripe nor green
at fourteen-
limbo of woman/girl.
He was twenty two,
blonde curly hair,
biceps the size of water balloons,
a tattoo in red and blue,
that spelled *Sheila,* framed by a heart.
He was an ex-con who had done time
for breaking and entering.
Taking a minor across state lines
didn't seem much like a felony to him.
We flew from Denver to Oklahoma
on a night I was supposed to fly
to visit my brother.
It was only a matter of hours before
my parents knew I was missing.
Runaway.
He was through with me quickly;
a teenage girl who didn't have the skills
to defend herself from grown men
was a liability.
He called my parents
and arranged to send me home –
a midnight flight.
Back in my own room
with the four poster bed and ruffles,
stuffed animals and a vanity-
in that mirror
I put on bright red lipstick and blew kisses
to my innocence.

Lower Middle Class

Waiting to hear my name called.
The captains picking their teams,
I'll take Jacob,
I'll take Alan,
I'll take Cassandra...

Feeling more dejected,
rejected at every name.
I pray silently that there
will be a place for me.
Will I be called last?
A left over, no one really wants
but has to play with.

These chips in my psyche
come early in life
and I learn
to earn favor
you must be athletic,
attractive,
or rich-
Your powerful parents able to throw
the best birthday party.

I'm a railroad worker's kid-
a welder's only daughter.
I'm ragged around the hem
of my hand-me-downs.

Something I Found

At twenty-three, I was visiting my dad, in the small town where I grew up. The morning after a football game, we walked to the stadium, and in each row between the seats we looked for items lost by the people who sat on the metal benches the night before. There were discarded cups and candy wrappers. There were pieces of orange and black streamers, and part of a paper sign that read, "Go Tig," the "ers" missing from the full word, Tigers. I found a leather necklace with a silver star and moon pendant. My dad found a green pocket knife. We both found quarters, dimes, nickels and pennies. As we crossed the field on our way home, my dad asked if I remembered searching the stands after games when I was a child. I told him I did. "Yep, we were white trash," he said. I stopped for a moment, because it was the first time I realized that we were not explorers looking for lost treasures in the sand of the desert or in the depth of the sea.

BROKEN UNION

Spoiled Sacrament

My wedding day
dressed in white,
the front of my hair tied back,
a veil covering my face-
ghostly beauty.

Someone put, "help" on the bottom of
Sammy's left shoe
and, "me" on the right shoe.
When we knelt at the altar
and the soles of his feet were visible
everyone laughed.

On our way out of the church,
the cross behind us,
my uncle picked up a metal pail
full of rice and poured it over my head.
Little white sticks were in my mouth,
my ears,
my bra padded with them.

In our honeymoon suite
our wedding party
had thrown cheese all over the floor,
and turned the thermostat up to high.
Yellow goo
met our bare feet.

Short sheeted.
Bubbles overflowing
from the Jacuzzi.

I wasn't in the mood
to give myself to you further.
You said it was the worst wedding night,
as if you had some memory to compare it to.

Once My Fisherman

You cast me into the dark waters-
Alone.
Depression had overtaken me.
An imposter
sleeping in our bed.
One who was heavy, sullen, sunken.
The lures you used to tie
and try and catch me:
shiny, bright, new,
no longer interested you.
When the doctor said I needed you
the most
to steady my pole,
weight my line,
hook up a red and white bobber
to float me,
until the medication did its duty.
You placed a gun at the side of our bed
next to my head
hoping I would give in and lose
all of my tackle.
Standing by that stream
where we once dreamed
we loved each other.

Tying the Knot

We tried the single sheet bend,
The double sheet bend,
The double eye knot,
The sliding overhead knot,
The round-turn fishhook tie,
The figure eight knot,
The half-blood knot,
The jansik special,
The homer rhode loop,
The improved clinch or pandre knot,
The jam knot with an extra tuck,
The clinch-on shank,
The nail loop,
The loop knot,
The double loop clinch knot,
The salmon hook knot,
The overhead dropper tie,
The perfection loop knot,
The extension blood knot,
The emergency dropper knot,
The improved dropper loop.
We tied them, tried them all
and then cut each other loose.

One Foot Here, One Foot There

I have been on the inside:
One of the popular girls
that gets invited to the sleepovers
and birthday parties.
I have been on the outside:
A bad girl
that dates the long-haired boy,
smokes cigarettes,
cuts school to drink coffee
at Denny's.
I have lived on both sides
Of the track:
Uptown
and downtown.
I have eaten meat
and given it up
for ten years.
I have voted
Democrat
and Republican.
I have succeeded
and I have failed.
I have given up
and given in.
I have danced
and I have waited at the edge
of the room watching others dip
to the music.
I have been single
and I have been married.
I have been frightened
and I have been courageous.
I have been well
and I have been ill.
I have been depressed

and I have been elated.
I have laughed
and I have cried.
I have walked
and I have fallen down.
These things tend to go
round and round.
It's the sound of someone
busy living
while the body gets closer
to dying.

All our Lives Boxes

Boxed in by the car you drive.
Boxed in by the friends you have.
Boxed in by the color of your skin.
Boxed in by going to college.
Boxed in by not going to college.
Boxed in by your life partner.
Boxed in by the possibility of parenthood.
Boxed in by your buying power.
Boxed in by your boss.
Boxed in by your job.
Boxed in by unemployment.
Boxed in by television.
Boxed in by the house you buy.
Boxed in by your neighborhood.
Boxed in by your health.
Boxed in by your illness.
Boxed in by your mind.
Boxed in by a coffin
for the final time.

HOSPITALS
AND
STIGMA

The Hospital is all White

They should have known
how it looks
how it ticks
and how it tocks.
Even the clock
can become suspect
in a plot to kill me.

Days after drugs
I become agreeable
And I am invited
to arts and crafts.

What I make resembles
a second grader's Mother's Day gift.
A glob of melted plastic
glued to a magnet
and the nurses say,
"That's good, that's really good."

Rest? This is No Resort

The bathroom is communal,
dull and yellow. The tile,
white and blue checked.
I wouldn't be here,
clever as I am
about the laws
that govern the mentally ill.
But for a moment
there was a slight
opening,
a break,
a window,
in my psychosis
that allowed me to see
I needed help.
Locked doors behind me
I'm no longer free.
Not allowed with other patients-
too disruptive,
can't be trusted.
A cold bare mattress to lie on.
The nurse angry.
I don't trust the sheets.
This is paranoia,
full blown.

Don't Stuff Me into an Antique Container

People like me are in boxes
shaped as stigma.
Everyone knows what it looks like
to be insane.
There are two choices:
Homeless and talking to voices
that can't be seen, and
institutionalized
in rooms without glass or sharp objects.
Against the air stream of a fan
I go on by the side of my
husband.
I am the woman next to you
at the grocery store.
The woman at the magazine stand
glancing over articles.
The woman at the gym
with a headset.
It's uncomfortable
to know you can't point out crazy
that's because we aren't.
We are every day
people like you
who have been stuffed in a too small
container
outdated and mislabeled.
It's time to open the lid
and let us out
so we can live
life
unhindered by four sides.

A Mass Grave

Where do the voices go
when I die?
Do they go to torture
some other victim of madness?
Does the man on the street
yelling
hear the same voices I do?
Is it all the same spirit,
these disembodied voices
controlling human beings?
I hope that when I die,
they die with me
so there will be less
voices heard
in the minds
of others.

Lebensunwert (Life Unworthy of Life)

It was like a train
with no brakes.

It started with sterilization:
schizophrenics,
the delayed,
deformed.

Then the architecture
of how best to kill them-
driving them around in a van
pumped full of gas.

Trial and error turned into showers.
They were bussed to warehouses
and told they needed to be washed down.

When the doors closed-
gas instead of water.

The fires where the bodies
were burned.

The towns surrounding the tortured looks
of people poisoned
could smell the hell of it.

This was the beginning of the Final Solution,
that would be perfected on the most vulnerable
and then used against the Jews,

and this is news
for those of us who would have been
part of the experiment.

Searching for Direction: East and West

I have visited Sufis
Yogis
And therapists
Searching for answers
To my illness
I have meditated
Prayed
Chanted
Posed
And talked
And experienced the physical side of enlightenment
I found no suitable answers
Except schizophrenia
I'll keep popping pills
And visiting psychiatrists
They are the only ones
Who lead me hand in hand
To inner peace

Watching the Homeless

People on the street
Talking to voices only they hear
Clothes with deep dark stains
That never will come out
Smelling like urine and alcohol
Matted hair
And missing teeth
Long toe nails and blackened feet
There I go
There I am
In another life
Unpredictable this illness
In another day
Right now living like a queen in comparison
A pillow holds and comforts my head
Water washes me clean
I am frightened of what I see
Knowing always
That could be me

All Alone

It's a private thing
This illness
Much like a letter
That no one else is allowed to open
It is addressed to me
The symptoms are at times public
But not the voices
The voices speak to me alone
And they are the sound of madness
Shouting or whispering or demanding
Even doctors can't share or taste it fully
Holding my hand they lead me down the path
But I know in a breath they'll be gone
Sharing only a slice
Of a delayed darkness

A Small Piece Doesn't Make the Whole

Yes, I have schizophrenia
But it is in last place
With the woman
I have become
Strong
Resilient
Creative
Powerful
Those characteristics
Are my legacy
I am a garden in full bloom
A river with wild rapids
A tree with deep roots
My illness is only a shadow
Hidden in the attic
Far from the whole of me

Cut Off Mid-Sentence

I had so much potential
As a young woman
A promising career
A poet's mind
Until psychosis
Crashed in like a car
Hitting a building
At high speed
Ripping a hole
All the way through
And exposing the center
It has taken two decades
To get back
To where I was
And I'm so far behind now
No roads will allow
Me to catch up
I must start over
And look at what is facing
Ahead

Becoming Invisible

It never would have occurred to me that I would become one of the invisibles while sitting in my doctor's office. If I was begging on the street, talking to voices no one else hears, or yelling at people passing by then I could possibly understand the avoidance, the lack of eye contact, the pretending that I don't exist, but I was sitting, with hair and make-up done, in my jeans and tank top, holding a manuscript, looking like a middle-class, middle-age housewife visiting her shrink.

I knew it was over when they started talking about the Colorado massacre. I knew it was only a matter of time before they said it. Yes, there it is, right behind crazy and orange hair – schizophrenic. It is the only time I hear the word used widely in public, when there is a tragedy and someone shoots a large number of people.

That is when I became invisible for the first time. I must be invisible. I am waiting in my psychiatrist's office. I am listening to the receptionist and the security guard talk about crazy people, and how the shooter of all those innocent people must be schizophrenic because of his orange hair. The receptionist says something that makes me know that I have changed from human being to something lowly, difficult, and unlovely, she says, "Believe me, I know, I work HERE don't I?" In response to the security guard talking about recognizing, "those" people when you see them.

The point is not lost on me. They don't recognize me. I have paranoid schizophrenia, and I am holding a manuscript that I wrote, ready to submit to a magazine and reveal my diagnosis to the world. I look at the pages and I try to focus on the words I wrote exposing my secret to the world. So, this is what it is going to be like when I go public? I am going to be invisible like so many other mentally ill people? Dear God, is it worth it to tell my story? Can I handle this avoidance and total disregard for my humanity?

My psychiatrist steps out and calls me into her office. I read her the manuscript. I tell her I am going public. I tell her I am afraid of the stigma, but I won't be the first or last to experience it. I tell her about the security guard and the receptionist. I think I see anger on her face for the first time ever. I find comfort in her anger, because it shows understanding and compassion. I change my mind, I am not invisible. I am a ghost that only certain people can see.

EVERYDAY LIFE

Living with Mental Illness

I am strong
I am brave
I have strength
And courage
I wake every day
With an enormous
Obstacle in my path
Called schizophrenia
It does no good to rail against it
I must accept it
Move to the side
And carry on

Mixing up Health

Measuring the flour, measuring the oil, and separating the sunflower yellow yolk from the mostly clear whites of the egg, I am baking another cake, one of five I will bake while the voices tell me I am a healer and whoever eats my food will overcome sickness and be made well. The voices tell me I am Jesus. I am a Shaman. I am powerful. The ingredients and my intentions mixed together will sooth, mend, stitch up, and cure. I try to pour positive thoughts into the batter: thoughts of love, health, wholeness and peace while the voices tell me to add fresh jam, strawberries, or chocolate chips.

As the cakes come out of the oven and are completely cool, I begin to frost them thinking of my neighbors, who I have been bringing cakes to every day for three weeks; lemon, chocolate, vanilla, strawberry and angel food. I give a fourth of a cake to the mailman Monday through Saturday because he is going through treatment for colon cancer. The voices tell me he will need a lot of cake to cure it.

I bake cakes this way for two months. Someone is always ringing my door bell to return an empty plate. The hallways of the apartment smell thick with fresh baked goods. I know most people in the building by name. I rarely smile because I am distracted by the constant sound of the voices, but people think I am nice because I have become the cake lady. One man that works from home comes over every day at 2:00 pm for a homemade latte and a slice of cake.

One day in mid-August, the voices turn on me. I am no longer a healer. I must die. I must die by my own hand. So far, I have been able to keep the voices hidden from my husband, but now I am frightened. I call him at work and tell him I am very sick and that I need to go to the hospital. He needs to take the bus home from National City and I wonder if I will hurt myself before he gets home.

He takes me to the emergency room. The psychiatrist, an older man, is kind. He talks to me like I am sane, without the least bit of condescension in his voice. He addresses me directly and not in the third person which is so often the case. He says he is comfortable increasing my medication. I am thankful. I am hopeful. I pray that the voices will stop now that they have turned from spiritual to terrifying.

Over the next couple of days the voices begin to subside. I hear them residually from listening to them so intently and following their direction for so long. Within a week, I am clear minded. The voices have gone to the mind of another. I pray the person who houses them will be safe.

The hallways no longer have the smell of fresh baked goods. The last of my plates gets returned. I no longer bake cakes and the most curious thing of all is no one asks why. The cake lady becomes their average neighbor sometimes exchanging a hello or good-bye, and lemon chocolate, vanilla, strawberry, and angel food are no longer on anyone's tongue.

Poisonous Thoughts

Looking at the menu that lists mostly meat and seafood, I choose a quinoa dish with a black bean hummus on a bed of lettuce with flatbread and chutney. I ask my husband what he is having and he says, "The pasta."

Our server, a young woman, with deeply colored tattoos completely covering what is exposed of one arm, and plugs the size of dimes in her ears, comes to our table with a big smile and nice straight white teeth. She puts down two glasses of ice water and asks if we have had time to look over the menu. We thank her for the water and my husband asks if they have a Stone IPA. She says they do, so he orders one along with both of our dinners.

This is no special occasion: we eat out all the time. The choice not to have children has caused us some heartache but it allows us to spend our money more freely than our friends who are putting their kids through college. Because we can, we love to try new restaurants.

We are both really hungry and wish out loud to one another that this was one of the many restaurants that served up bread, salsa and chips, or crackers and hummus before the meal. We would have ordered an appetizer but then there is always way too much food and no matter what they say, leftovers do not taste as good the second day. The kitchen seems slow, and because I get grumpy from not eating every two hours, we are trying to engage in small talk. The words are coming out in bits and pieces and we can't get a conversation going.

When our food does arrive, it is beautifully presented on the plates. My husband's pasta has sauce spread into a red swirly design all along the edge of his plate and my meal is stacked in colorful layers and I can't wait to take the first bite, and so I pick up my fork and knife and cut a piece slightly larger than my mouth and begin to chew. The whole evening changes in that moment.

My illness is upon us and my mind has become a battleground between rational and irrational thought. What started it was that first bite that should have been delicious, that should have instantly hit my taste buds with a wide range of flavors, and should have immediately went to work on my low blood sugar, but what happened instead was that first bite had something in it that I had never tasted before. It could have been a combination of spices, it could have been an unfamiliar herb, and it could have been salt from the Himalayas for all I knew because what it actually was doesn't matter.

The fact that I couldn't recognize the taste is what caused the thought tremor. In order to avoid a full-blown thought earthquake, I put down my fork and tell my husband, "Something tastes funny." This is his cue to try my food. Usually, if he tries the food I am struggling with, I will accept his opinion or analysis of it and get past the thought that it is poisoned and be able to resume eating. He tastes it and says, "This tastes fine," which is his way of saying, "I know you think this is poisonous but I just ate a huge bite of it and I didn't choke, start to bleed out of my mouth, nose or eyes, or in other words, die. Try to enjoy your meal."

I'm sure if they took a scan of my brain at moments like these they would see colors light up in areas of the brain that are normally dark. I try to reason my way back to the food in front of me. I tell myself, "I have paranoid schizophrenia and this is just a symptom of my illness. Everything will be fine. No one poisoned the food." My brain responds by saying, "Certainly no one poisoned it intentionally but what if they spilled bleach in it by accident in the kitchen? The unfamiliar taste could have been bleach. Yes, it smells like bleach."

My husband sees that I am losing this battle that rages on in my mind even as he wishes that tonight his opinion would have comforted me enough to alleviate my fears. He really wants his pasta, but he says, "Would you like to eat this instead?"

"Yes, thank you," I say a little nervous and defeated. He is so used to giving me his food; food that he wants for his self that disappointment doesn't even register on his face. My husband takes a bite of the quinoa and I poke at the pasta with my fork. He tries to make us both laugh. We must laugh hard and frequently to avoid being swallowed by my fears.

Overcoming Obstacles

I am not a genius or a madwoman. It is true, I have paranoid schizophrenia, but I'm not creating breakthrough math formulas, or plotting to shoot up a movie theater. When I go downtown I don't stand on street corners and talk to people only I can see or hear. I don't spend my days in a tinfoil hat, and I don't believe the numerous fillings from cavities are transmitting anything with the exception of bacteria to the rest of my mouth.

I am fairly certain that I have more in common with you than we have differences. I belong to a political party although there are times when I vote across party lines if the candidate appears to stand for what I believe in. There are television shows that I like to binge watch, one being *Orange is the New Black*. I also love a good documentary. I have spinach in my smoothie every morning but Oreo cookies or popcorn are what I take to bed.

I know it probably won't sit well with the stereotypes, and it might make you a little uncomfortable as some of your old beliefs are to be pried loose, but I am married and perfectly capable of being a loving and supportive partner. I like to bring my husband coffee in bed. I also take him to the doctor any time he comes down with the flu, because I am slightly over protective and he has an autoimmune disease. I can handle all of the grocery shopping, although I'm not much of a cook. I can bake better than most of my friends. I don't consider anything out of a box real baking.

You are probably wondering how I got diagnosed with paranoid schizophrenia if I think I am so much like you. At twenty-eight years old I became psychotic. At the time, I thought everyone was out to get me. I believed I was in danger and safety was something so elusive I couldn't even find it in the comfort of sleep, mostly because I wasn't sleeping more than an hour at a time. I feared everything I was eating was poisoned. I thought I would be raped and tortured. I was terrified. I couldn't sit still. I paced. I ran. I tried to jump through windows. I barricaded my mother in a room. I smoked two or more packs of cigarettes a day.

During the time that I was psychotic you would have felt cozy and comfortable with my behavior because it was within the normal ideas about mental illness. I was in a psych ward. I was in a locked room. I did things that were rational only to me, and I couldn't hold a conversation. I was heavily medicated and was sent to craft classes where I made refrigerator magnets that looked like the work of a third grader. I was trapped in my mind. I was contained both figuratively and literally. I had too many cares and I wasn't free.

It hurt my self-esteem to have to live with the new me, the one that was mentally ill, and I didn't always follow the doctor's directions for my medication. I ended up psychotic again less than a year later. This time the voices came. If you have never heard voices before, let me tell you at first you are confused by their presence. At least I was. I thought I was hearing directly from God or angels. I thought I was having a religious experience and that the voices were teaching me to overcome my fears.

I stood on the railing of the Tacoma Narrows Bridge, hundreds of feet above the Puget Sound until a stranger took my hand and pulled me to safety. I took all of my medication and another stranger found me passed out on the side of the road and waited with me until an ambulance arrived. They had to jump start my heart. Two strangers, two suicides attempts, one life saved.

I took my treatment more seriously after hearing voices that told me to kill myself. I didn't want to die. I didn't want to hear voices that were out to injure me. I was terrified that maybe someday they would be successful in killing me or hurting someone else. I took my medication regularly, until I didn't.

During my next psychotic episode the voices were back and I was certain that I was Jesus. I walked sixteen hours through the streets of Los Angeles, believing I was the Son of God. I perched on the corner of buildings high above the city, believing that if I fell, God would protect me from harm. When I walked through dangerous neighborhoods, the voices pointed out the evil. I thought I saw devils. I thought I saw demons. I was convinced that I needed to get back to Washington State. My husband and I drove to my parents' house in just under twenty four hours. This time, I took the medication exactly the way it was prescribed and I was fine for eight years. I worked. I made friends. I kept house. I completed a leadership training program for the city we lived in, and I sat on boards for the city council. I felt like I had made it. I had built a successful life despite my mental illness.

I was doing so well that the psychiatrist who had been treating me over six years, said there was no way I was mentally ill. He believed my psychotic episodes were due to trauma, and that as long as life was good, my mind would remain sound. I could be counted on. I was rational. I was funny. We believed I was cured.

It took a year without medication to decompensate completely. I was psychotic again, and this time there were voices that were so strong and powerful that I couldn't even talk to other people because they were so distracting. "Divorce your husband," they said. "Go live at the beach." "Run away. Run. Run." I got in the car and drove. "They are listening to you. That radio is bugged. They can hear you and see you through the TV."

My husband tracked me by our credit card. I stayed at the beach in a little motel for a week or more. I finally went home. My husband found me a psychiatrist and I started on medication, but the voices continued for six months. We barely made it, my husband and me. We had just moved to San Diego, he had a new job to be concerned about, and a wife that was far more interested in voices from places she didn't know than the voices of people standing next to her. After months of being psychotic, the voices turned menacing and again, they told me to kill myself.

Something inside of me woke up. Something didn't want to die. I called my husband and said, "Please help. I need to see a doctor again." He came home from work as fast as he could and took me to the emergency room. The doctor there was comfortable increasing my medication. In two days, only echoes of the voices were left. Once again, I had to rebuild my life.

That was eight years ago. My mind is silent now. Occasionally I hear a song run through my mind and it will play over and over again for what seems like days, but there are no voices. No voice. Only a white blank slate, a board I fill with writing. I have symptoms of my illness because I have paranoid schizophrenia, but the symptoms are only obvious to those I trust. Occasionally I can't eat food because I believe it is poisoned. Occasionally I have overwhelming fears that I am dying. There are times when I don't trust anyone but my husband. Even though Paris is my favorite city, I don't like to travel because I am afraid that my medication will be lost or stolen. I must have my medication, every day at breakfast and dinner. I live around my medication schedule. The pills are my security blanket, helping me to live a normal life. I want a normal life. I love the mundane.

Before I go to bed each night, I ask my husband the same question, "Guess what I am excited about for tomorrow?" He knows me so well, he can often guess. "Your morning coffee," is always his first answer. If I shake my head, "No," he tries again with, "The mail." Those two things are highlights of every day, but occasionally it will be something unique, like making a deadline or hearing from a magazine about some writing I submitted. I enjoy the simple things, a call from a friend, or a walk to the park. These things that seem so small to other people keep me going and make my heart full. I don't have a complicated life. It is simple. I am extremely happy. You know what? Maybe, we don't have as much in common as I thought. I don't know, if you take normalcy for granted, we are not so similar, because I relish in it. I have paranoid schizophrenia, and I love my life.

I am a flower that has been fortunate enough to bloom.

Acknowledgments

Thank you to the publications that first published these works:

Freedom of Speech was first published in *Transition*, Summer 2014.

Coming Out in Light was first published in *Sundays at Liberty Station*, 2015.

Tying the Knot was first published in *Structo*, Issue 13 Spring/Summer 2015. It is forthcoming in the *Reader*, April 2015.

When Dinner Bleeds was first published in *Serving House Journal*, Issue 9, Spring 2014.

Something I found was first published in *Sundays at Liberty Station*, 2015.